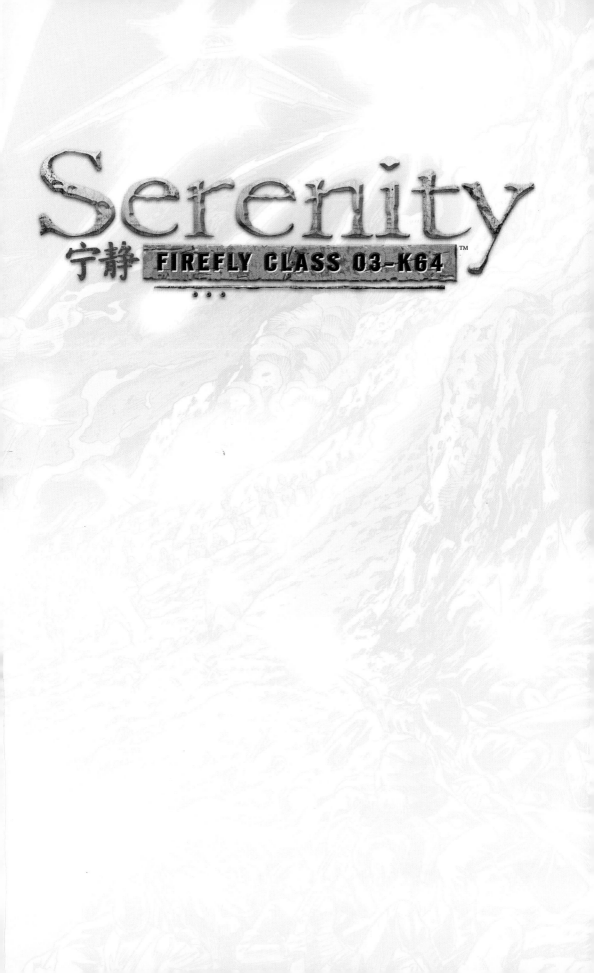

Serenity

宁静 **FIREFLY CLASS 03-K64** ™

Serenity
宁静 · FIREFLY CLASS 03-K64 ™

——— THOSE LEFT BEHIND ———

STORY
JOSS WHEDON & BRETT MATTHEWS

SCRIPT
BRETT MATTHEWS

ART
WILL CONRAD

COLORS
LAURA MARTIN

LETTERS
MICHAEL HEISLER

COVER ART
ADAM HUGHES

DARK HORSE BOOKS

PRESIDENT & PUBLISHER
MIKE RICHARDSON

EDITORS
SCOTT ALLIE & SIERRA HAHN

ASSISTANT EDITOR
FREDDYE LINS

COLLECTION DESIGNER
JUSTIN COUCH

SPECIAL THANKS TO CINDY CHANG AT UNIVERSAL STUDIOS
AND MATT DRYER AND DAVE MARSHALL AT DARK HORSE COMICS.

———————————

NEIL HANKERSON Executive Vice President • TOM WEDDLE Chief Financial Officer • RANDY STRADLEY Vice President of Publishing • MICHAEL MARTENS Vice President of Book Trade Sales • ANITA NELSON Vice President of Business Affairs • DAVID SCROGGY Vice President of Product Development • DALE LAFOUNTAIN Vice President of Information Technology • DARLENE VOGEL Senior Director of Print, Design, and Production • KEN LIZZI General Counsel • MATT PARKINSON Senior Director of Marketing • DAVEY ESTRADA Editorial Director • SCOTT ALLIE Senior Managing Editor CHRIS WARNER Senior Books Editor • DIANA SCHUTZ Executive Editor • CARY GRAZZINI Director of Print and Development • LIA RIBACCHI Art Director • CARA NIECE Director of Scheduling

Serenity: Firefly Class 03-K64 Volume 1—Those Left Behind

Published by Dark Horse Books
A division of Dark Horse Comics, Inc.
10956 SE Main Street
Milwaukie, OR 97222

DarkHorse.com

To find a comics shop in your area, call the
Comic Shop Locator Service toll-free at (888) 266-4226.

First hardcover edition: November 2007
Second hardcover edition: August 2012

ISBN 978-1-59582-914-6

1 3 5 7 9 10 8 6 4 2
Printed in the USA

Art by Adam Hughes

Art by John Cassaday
Colors by Laura Martin

INTRODUCTION

When I was very young, before I could read, I remember being interested in comic books. Our bedtime was not negotiable, but we could delay "lights out" for another half hour if we read anything. I mostly looked at the pictures; I could make out "a" and "the," and then simply tried to piece together a story. I could tell that Jughead liked to eat, Archie was broke, Betty was nice, and Veronica was mean. There are only so many times you can read the same ones, though, so my dad would take my brother and me to Whyte Avenue. Not too far down from Uncle Albert's Pancake House (burned down since then) was the Wee Book Inn, a store that had an odor a bit like someone's grandmother's house. Not mine, but someone's. I remember the dirty orange carpet, frayed and ragged. The wooden shelves were tall and packed with worn covers of books read many times over. Pages were yellowed and paperbacks had arched spines like old swaybacked horses. It was an old-folks' home for secondhand books, with that smell of old newsprint and slightly musty wood. There were stacks of magazines with fat, contented cats sleeping on them that you could pet without fear of being scratched. If ever there was a mystical "Ye Olde Magic Shoppe" in my life, this was it. It was a trading post for old books, and more importantly, comics. My dad would have us bring all the comics we could bear to part with, and we would watch as the clerk would shuffle through them, calculating their value. I felt as though I was in the days of the Klondike, come down from my claim in the hills and waiting for the assayer to separate the fool's gold from the real thing. His appraisal would determine how many secondhand comics we could walk away with. Always fewer than what we came in with, but my pops would pull out his wallet, careful to make sure we never left with a smaller stack. Comics were our treasure, our booty, and we would rush up to our rooms and file them away carefully on our very own spinning comic rack.

Soon, Archie, Dot, and Richie Rich gave way to Spider-Man, Captain America, X-Men, and Alpha Flight (Canada's very own superteam). Now, around this time, my memories blur a bit, but what I remember is this—I wanted to be a superhero. My brain was constantly calculating my supermoves, my supercostume, what powers I would have, how I would use them, and with whom I would share my incredible secret. My brother was in, my parents were out—lest they force me to use my newfound abilities on chores. There were, however, no radioactive spiders available to me, no toxic-waste sites, and I found out very quickly, despite my brother's urging, that jumping off the garage roof with two kites to sweep over the neighborhood didn't work. When the price of comics increased, so did my interest in girls and cars, and my treasure was relegated to the darkness of the crawlspace of our house, carefully packed in plastic bags and taped twice, not once. My desire to be a superhero, however, never abated. I couldn't help but think about how being able to fly and being bulletproof would help me in any endeavor I chose.

And then there was Joss. I met him in a small, dimly lit office, where he regaled me with tales of adventure, swashbuckling, shooting, spaceships, and narrow escapes. Um, where do I sign? He gave me a new identity, a costume, a gun, and a long brown duster for a cape. I remember that meeting so well; it was like a superhero "origin" issue. I remember Joss looking at Polaroid photos of my first costume fitting, holding up the one with the duster and gun, saying, "Action figure, anyone?"

Never in my wildest. Like some sort of superteam benefactor, Joss made superheroes out of all of us, complete with a superhideout spaceship. During filming, we'd all retreat to our dressing-room trailers and emerge like supermen with our alter egos. The boots, the suspenders, gun holstered low on my hip . . . with a flick and a spin of that wicked-awesome coat over my shoulders, I became someone else.

So, I guess the message I want to leave you with is this: What you hold in your hand is not just a comic. It is much more. It is a handbook. It is a guide. It is reference material for when you become a superhero. I have found the secret, you see. To become a superhero, all you have to do is want it badly enough, and comics are the fuel to that fire.

Incidentally, you hold in your hand my favorite (*favourite* for Canadians) . . . comic . . . ever.

Dark Horse and our cover artists have given us a great introduction to Joss's world of comic action heroes. They amazed us from the first issue, packed with shooting, crashing, punching, and splatting. Thank you, everyone. I'll be placing this series in my comic-book rack, just as soon as I get this home. It will be wrapped and double taped.

—Nathan Fillion

Art by J. G. Jones
Colors by Laura Martin

GONNA TAKE A WHILE FOR THE STINK OF THIS TO PASS.

JUST A SEWER, JAYNE.

WEREN'T TALKING ABOUT THE SEWER.

NOW AIN'T THE TIME, JAYNE.

UNDERSTOOD?

WELL, YOU JUST BE SURE AND SAY *WHEN.*

SO... THE JOB'S BUST AND I HAVE NO DOUBT OTT AND HIS HAVE ALREADY MADE IT OFF WORLD, AND EVEN LESS THAT THEY DID US THE FAVOR OF DOING SO QUIETLY.

IT'S A FAIR BET HE'S TURNED THE WHOLE DAMN PLANET ON TO US, SO WE'D DO BEST TO SHUT OUR MOUTHS, KEEP OUR HEADS LOW, AND SEE IF WE CAN'T OBTAIN OURSELVES--

SSKKKRREEEEEEEE

Art by Bryan Hitch
Colors by Laura Martin

Art by Jo Chen

GET HER FUELED, WASH.

WITH DIRT? WITH *CHEAP* DIRT?

THAT'S ABOUT ALL THIS IS GONNA GET US...

GET HER FUELED IN AS MUCH AS YOU CAN.

INARA'S GOT A SCHEDULE TO KEEP.

MAL!

THE REST OF YOU ARE FREE TO TAKE A WALKABOUT, DO WHAT YOU NEED TO DO, BUT BE BACK ON THE SHIP COME SUNDOWN...

A BLINK'S AN AWFUL LONG TIME WHEN YOU'RE ON THE GROUND.

WE'RE NOT REQUIRIN' A LECTURE ON THE SUBJECT. OR HAD YOU NOT NOTICED THE *COLOR* THE CAPTAIN AND I ARE PARTIAL TO WEARING?

HERE'S WHAT YOU AND THE HISTORY BOOKS *DON'T* KNOW.

WHAT THE BATTLE OF STURGES WAS FOUGHT FOR -- WHAT ALL THEM BOYS AND GIRLS *DIED* FOR -- WAS A BOATLOAD OF *CASH.*

A BOATLOAD OF CASH THAT'S STILL THERE.

THE *COORDINATES,* MAL.

TAKE YOU RIGHT TO THE BATTLEFIELD -- AND THE STASH OF *REAL* THEM *BROWNCOATS* GOT BUTCHERED OVER. IT'S JUST SITTING THERE FOR YOU, OR SOMEONE NEAR ENOUGH YOU, TO SNATCH IT UP.

LESS MY *PERCENTAGE,* OF COURSE.

WHAT DO YOU SAY?

I SAY I'LL THINK ABOUT IT.

NOW GET OFF MY SHIP BEFORE THE STAIN SETS...

"YOU'VE GOT A LONG WALK AHEAD OF YOU."

AS I'M SURE YOU'VE ALL SUSSED FOR YOURSELVES...

WE'LL BE *TAKING* BADGER'S JOB.

ANYONE HAS A COMPLAINT, THEY'D BEST KNOW OF PAYING WORK TO GO ALONG WITH IT.

THIS IS *AFTER* YOU'VE DELIVERED ME TO MY DUTIES...

NO, IT IS DECIDEDLY NOT.

I CAN'T WAIT ON THIS, INARA, AND RUNNING A TAXI SERVICE DON'T FEED MOUTHS. FOR THE RECORD, THIS JOB IS IN THE SAME DIRECTION YOU'RE SO ANXIOUS TO GO, AND THE ONLY REASON WE'RE EVEN VENTURIN' TO SUCH A 什么工作都没有 CORNER OF SPACE IS *YOU.* STILL, I IMAGINE YOU'RE UPSET, AND I WANT YOU TO KNOW I'M...

THAT I WISH THINGS COULD BE *DIFFERENT.* IT'S JUST A DECISION I HAD TO MAKE.

YES, THE *ONLY* ONE YOU EVER DO.

PACK IT UP, BOYS. THERE'S ONLY ONE THING YOU NEED TO REMEMBER, WHEN WE GET THERE...

I'M THE ONE THAT KILLS REYNOLDS.

Art by Joe Quesada
Colors by Richard Isanove

Art by Sean Phillips

AIRLOCK ESTABLISHED.

PREPARE TO BREACH.

WHAT THE --

RIVER...?

INARA?

I'M SORRY TO BARGE IN, BUT IT'S RIVER. SHE HAD AN...EPISODE.

I WAS HOPING YOU COULD LOOK AFTER HER WHILE I RUN SOME TESTS.

OF COURSE I WILL.

YOU'LL HARDLY KNOW SHE'S HERE. SHE HASN'T SAID A WORD SINCE--

BELLY!

NOT YOURS, NOT HERS.

HERS...

YOU MISSED THIS ONE.

WASH, WE'RE HEADED BACK YOUR WAY. RAN INTO A BIT OF A PROBLEM.

I CAN BEAT IT...

I'M RUNNIN' OUTTA WAYS TO REWIRE HER, WASH. I'M A STEP AHEAD OF 'EM, BUT IT AIN'T GONNA LAST...

KEEP AT IT, KAYLEE.

THEY COME THROUGH, YOU GET YOURSELF TO INARA'S SHUTTLE.

SHE'LL KNOW WHAT THAT MEANS.

SHEPHERD --

PLEASE DON'T CALL ME THAT.

IT MAKES THIS HARDER...

WASH, WHAT THE HELL IS GOING ON OVER THERE?

I'D EXPLAIN, MAL, BUT I'M FLYING AT 不要命的速度 SPEED THROUGH A MESS OF POINTY STUFF AT THE MOMENT.

AND WHY THE HELL ARE YOU DOING THAT?!

JUST LOOKIN' FOR A GOOD FIT.

THERE. EVERYBODY HOLD ON...

我在前世一定惹到什么人了吧...

I'LL MISS YOU, INARA.

I KEEP COMING UP WITH ALL MANNER OF THINGS TO SAY BUT THAT'S WHAT THEY ALL MEAN, IT COMES RIGHT DOWN TO IT.

I DON'T WANT YOU TO --

AM I INTERRUPTING SOMETHING, CAPTAIN?

NOT THAT I KNOW WHAT THAT WOULD BE, YOU STANDING HERE ALONE IN THE MIDDLE OF THE NIGHT.

WE'RE IN SPACE, SHEPHERD. IT'S ALWAYS THE MIDDLE OF THE NIGHT.

WHAT'S ON YOUR MIND?

I'M LEAVING THE SHIP.

DON'T KNOW WHERE FOR JUST YET, BUT IT'S TIME FOR ME TO MOVE ON. I THOUGHT YOU SHOULD BE THE FIRST TO KNOW.

LOOK, SHEPHERD, .. I'LL MAKE THIS PLAIN...

IT DON'T MATTER TO ME THAT YOU HIT ME.

WHICH IS EXACTLY WHY I NEED TO BE AWAY FROM YOU.

BECAUSE SOONER OR LATER, IT WON'T MATTER TO ME, EITHER.

THOSE LEFT BEHIND
结尾

Serenity

宁静 **FIREFLY CLASS 03-K64** ™

The following section contains the preproduction memo "A Brief History of the Universe, Circa 2516 A.D." written by Joss Whedon for use during the *Serenity* motion picture.

The accompanying artwork, created by renowned comic-book artists Leinil Francis Yu (*X-Men*; *Superman: Birthright*) and Joshua Middleton (*NYX*; *Superman/Shazam: First Thunder*), was used as concept art during preproduction of the film *Serenity*. They also contributed variant covers to the comic-book series.

Left: River by
Joshua Middleton
Right: Simon by
Leinil Francis Yu

A BRIEF HISTORY OF THE UNIVERSE, Circa 2516 A.D.

By Joss Whedon

Earth-That-Was couldn't handle the growing population and resource needs of human-kind. Amazingly enough, instead of wiping itself out, the human race rose to the challenge of finding a new home for the species. A nearby star was located, home to dozens of planets and hundreds of moons, almost all of which had enough mass and solidity to be templates for new Earths. Through giant atmosphere processing plants, terraforming technologies, gravity regulation, and the introduction of every known form of Earthlife, each planet became its own little (or in some cases, huge) Earth. Every person willing and able to leave the Earth migrated to the new system. An entire generation never even saw the outside of a spaceship; the journey took so long. But the planets were ready for habitation (despite the odd quirk of nature or miscalculation on a few) and civilization as we knew it began to rebuild. The work started on the two largest, most central planets, SIHNON and LONDINIUM.

On Earth-That-Was, the two ruling powers were once known as America and China. Though their empires remained separate, the two powers worked together throughout the colonization process, their cultures—as so many had—melding at many levels. Londinium, called so after the Roman name for England's capital (a country long before annexed by America in a somewhat ironic reversal), represented what was once the

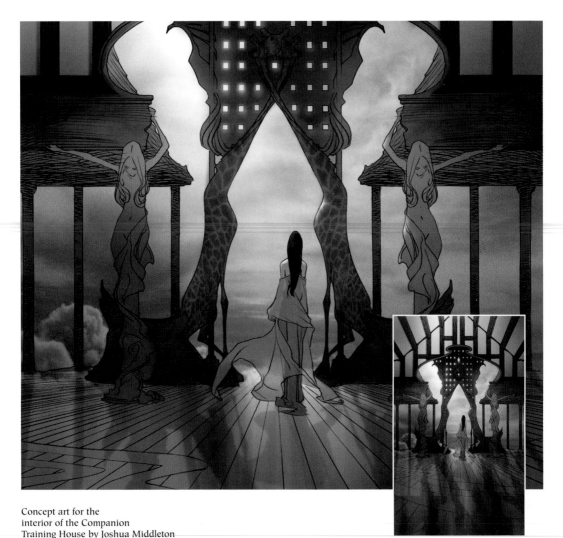

Concept art for the
interior of the Companion
Training House by Joshua Middleton

Concept art for the Companion
Training House set
high in the mountains by Joshua Middleton

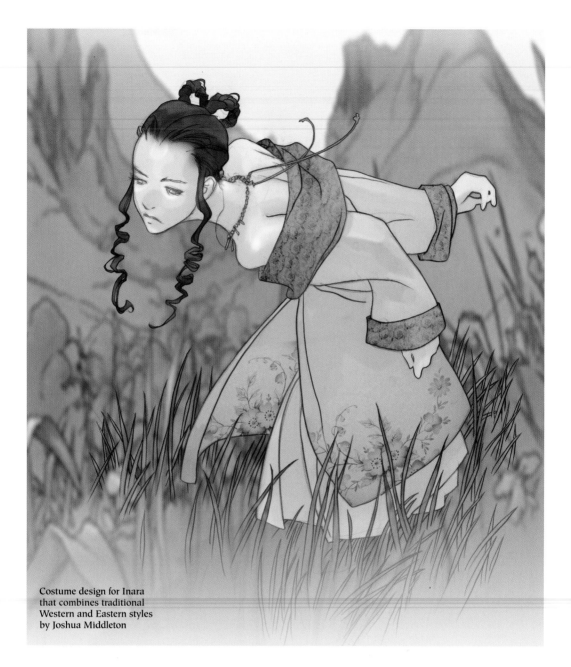

Costume design for Inara
that combines traditional
Western and Eastern styles
by Joshua Middleton

American Empire. Sihnon ("SEE-non," a bas-
tardization of Sino, our word for "Chinese") was
the new China, basically. These two powers, still
working in harmony, grew at once into the most
populous and advanced civilizations in the new
galaxy.

"Advanced" meant just that: these were
enlightened cultures, with respect for all non-
aggressive religious beliefs (though the main
religion on both planets was Buddhism). Liter-
acy levels were at 94 percent. Average lifespan
was 120. Public service was not law—it was simply an ingrained part of the people's ethos. And

pot was totally legal (though I probably won't
stress that. In fact, forget I said it). The point is,
certain social mores had evolved (whether for-
ward or backward is a matter of opinion) beyond
our modern conceptions. As, for example, sex.
Prostitution as we understand it had long since
been abolished by the legalization and strict fed-
eral regulation of the sex trade. "Companion"
houses were set up throughout the central planets. No house could ever be run by a man. No
Companion could ever be coerced into accepting
a client. Companions trained in all the arts; they
were extremely well schooled. They lived not

Costume design for Inara
by Joshua Middleton

Art by Joshua Middleton

Inara hairstyle concept art
by Joshua Middleton

New Mule concept art
by Leinil Francis Yu

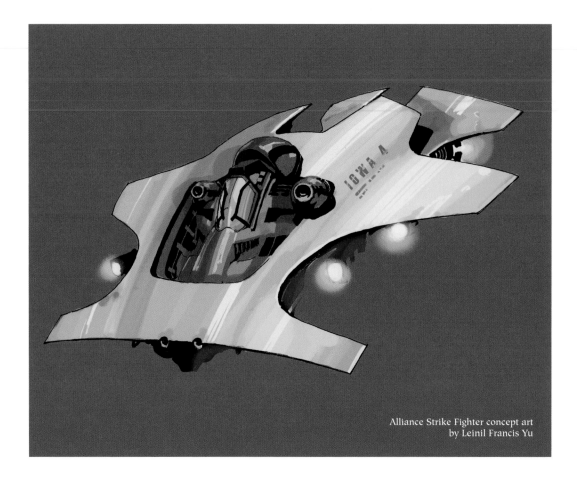

Alliance Strike Fighter concept art
by Leinil Francis Yu

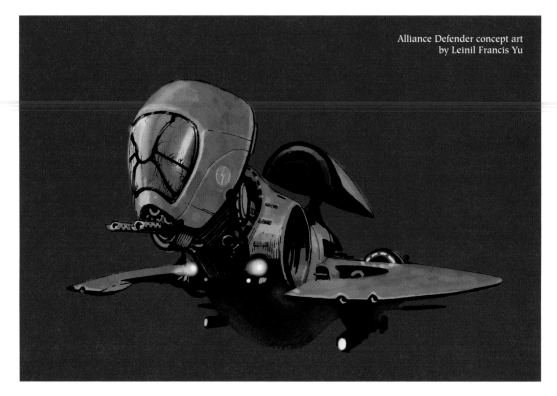

Alliance Defender concept art
by Leinil Francis Yu

unlike nuns, worked not unlike geishas, and often rose to political or social prominence when they retired.

Such was life on the central planets: among them Sihnon, Londinium, and Osiris (where Simon and River Tam grew up). On the outer planets, things were a mite different.

The thing is, we had enough worlds to go around, but not enough resources. And people didn't exactly stop making babies. The outer planets, the worlds and moons that hadn't been chosen to house the new civilization—they were the destination for the poorer, the more extreme, the pioneers. They traveled out to the nearest planet someone hadn't claimed yet and started turning their rockets into roofs. Building off whatever the land had been shaped to provide them with. Some of these people were brought near to savagery by the conditions they encountered. Some were just hard-working, independent folk who didn't want their lives mapped out for them before they'd lived them. Didn't

want convenience. Some were orthodox in their beliefs to the point where they were not comfortable among nonbelievers, and wanted worlds where they would not be slowly homogenized into the ruling society. And some had reason to avoid the law.

There were troubles. There were famines; there were wars—the human race didn't get better or smarter just 'cause they had made scientific leaps. Things were definitely more peaceful amongst the central planets, but that peace was bought at a price. Nothing resembling totalitarianism, but a certain regulation of existence that would not sit well with some. And even among these planets, conflicts over resources, trade, and political influence strained the civil relations of sister nations. In an effort to unite and quell this conflict, the central planets formed the ALLIANCE, a governing structure that unified them all under one governing body, the PARLIAMENT. The few members represented each planet, and worked in genuine harmony to

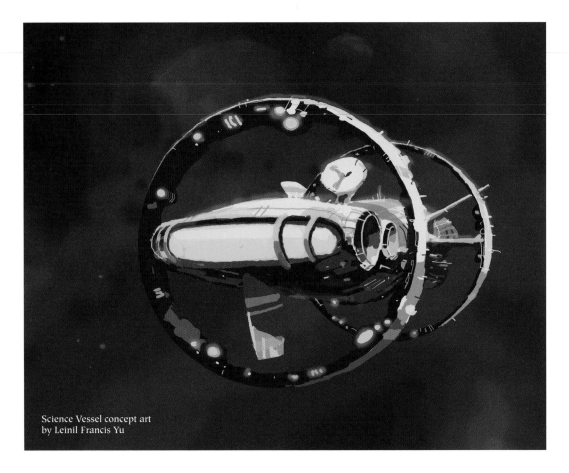

Science Vessel concept art
by Leinil Francis Yu

fulfill each planet's various needs, economically and politically. In harmony, and very often, in secrecy.

For we are nothing more than human, however high we reach. The Parliament ruled over the people with fairness and intelligence, but also with a strong army and a wary eye toward any insurrection. The MILITARY COUNCIL worked under the Parliament to deliver swift, effective control of any real unrest among them or their neighbors. And even beyond the knowledge of the Military Council were other bodies, secret bodies . . . human experimentation. Spies. Assassins. Schemes, secret up to the highest level, to get people to behave. To improve.

The real trouble started when the Alliance started to look beyond its borders to the worlds around them. Partially out of a desire to see life improved there (and it *was* often unnecessarily barbaric), to bring all the planets into the fold of enlightenment, and partially out of a simple imperialistic wish for control and need for resources offlimits to them, the Parliament—and the Allied planets as a whole—decided that *every* planet should become part of their program. Should be an Alliance planet, whether they wanted to or not.

The War for Unification was the most devastating in human history. Outer planets such as Hera (where the Battle of Serenity was fought), Persephone, and Shadow mustered forces—more than half volunteers—to stop what they felt to be nothing more than imperialist hegemony. For almost five years the war tore into the planets between the central ones and the rim worlds (fighting never reached such pissant moons as Whitefall or Beaumonde, nor did it ever touch Sihnon or Londinium, except in the odd protest or terrorist act). The forces of the Alliance had the technology and the weapons to overcome almost any foe. But they never expected the kind of resistance the other planets could provide. They did not expect so many men and women to still consider freedom worth dying for.

Malcolm Reynolds was on Shadow, living on the cattle ranch his mother ran, when he joined up.

Downed Science Vessel concept
art by Leinil Francis Yu

Reaver Destroyer Ship concept art
by Leinil Francis Yu

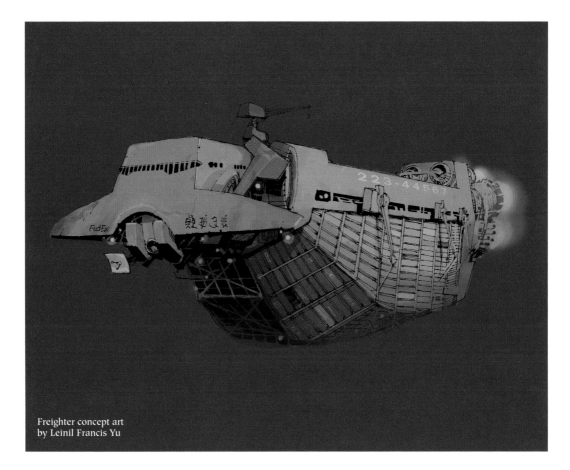

Freighter concept art
by Leinil Francis Yu

He was a smart kid but green. He joined out of belief and nothing more. Five years gone found his homeworld destroyed, his army beaten down, and every shred of belief ripped out of him. He had made sergeant by then, of the Fifty-seventh Overlanders. Would have gone higher if he had ever kept a single opinion to himself. But he wasn't in the war to get a title. He was there to fight, and in the Battle of Serenity, waged for seven grueling weeks on Hera, he fought like nobody else. Some say that valley was the bridge between the worlds, and that when it fell the Independents fell with it. Surely Mal believed it, for he and his held the valley for a good two weeks *after* the Independent High Command had already surrendered.

When it was all done, there was some talk of branding the "Browncoats" such as Mal who had held Serenity Valley as war criminals, since the war had officially ended. They were held in camps for a short time, but the Alliance considered it an important gesture to free them. The stain of criminality never left those few

thousand—but in some quieter circles, the legend of their tenacity made them heroes.

Among those few thousand was Corporal Zoe Alleyne, also of the Fifty-seventh Ovelanders. She had been career army, the opposite of Mal, but she had fought under him for the last two and a half years of the war, in more than a dozen campaigns. She also had the distinction of being the only other member of the Fifty-seventh to survive Serenity. When Mal decided to get himself a little transport ship and head out to the rim worlds, to work the planets the Alliance would not truly be able to control, to settle down never and draw breath free . . . it never occurred to her not to follow him. It also never occurred to her that they would hire a pilot as annoying as Hoban Washburne, or that she would fall so completely in love with him. They were married not a year after they met, an occurrence that Mal considered illadvised and slightly weird.

Wash turned out to be an extraordinary pilot, and they happened (it's a funny story) on a little prodigy of a mechanic, Kaywinnit Lee

Frye, known as Kaylee. As sweet and cheerful as she was mechanical, she found the opportunity to be chief engineer (a title she used only to herself) on a Firefly-class ship to be beyond her best imaginings. Most folk wouldn't look twice at a Firefly—it had since been replaced by sleeker, more efficient models, but she knew, as Mal did, that a Firefly could hold up where others would buckle . . . that she could get in and out of places other ships couldn't, and quickly too . . . that she was just right for the kind of jobs nobody was supposed to be doing anymore.

'Cause a lot of the work to be found on the border planets was crime, and that was no problem for Mal. He expected it, and he prepared for it. He found himself a great lug of a mercenary in Jayne Cobb: mean, untrustworthy, and indispensable. On the flip side, they actually landed a passenger who could lend them respectability: A first-rate Companion, Inara Serra, who had left House Madrassa on Sihnon to work independently. She never did say why.

Then one day they took on a Shepherd named Book and a young doctor from Osiris named Simon Tam, who had his sister River hidden in a cryogenic box for some damn reason. And that is, of course, another story.

ALSO FROM JOSS WHEDON

SERENITY VOLUME 1: THOSE LEFT BEHIND
SECOND EDITION HARDCOVER
Joss Whedon, Brett Matthews, and Will Conrad
ISBN 978-1-59307-846-1 $17.99

SERENITY VOLUME 2: BETTER DAYS AND
OTHER STORIES HARDCOVER
Joss Whedon, Patton Oswalt, Zack Whedon, Patric Reynolds and others
ISBN 978-1-59582-739-5 $19.99

SERENITY VOLUME 3: THE SHEPHERD'S TALE HARDCOVER
Joss Whedon, Zack Whedon, and Chris Samnee
ISBN 978-1-59582-561-2 $14.99

DR. HORRIBLE AND OTHER HORRIBLE STORIES
Joss Whedon, Zack Whedon, Joëlle Jones, and others
ISBN 978-1-59582-577-3 $9.99

MYSPACE DARK HORSE PRESENTS VOLUME 1
Featuring Sugarshock *by Joss Whedon and Fábio Moon*
ISBN 978-1-59307-998-7 $19.99

DOLLHOUSE VOLUME 1: EPITAPHS
Andrew Chambliss, Jed Whedon, Maurissa Tancharoen, and Cliff Richards
ISBN 978-1-59582-863-7 $18.99

FROM JOSS WHEDON